Dream
Power

Dream Power

Using Your Dreams to Empower Your Life

Laureli Blyth

BARNES
& NOBLE
BOOKS
NEW YORK

Contents

What is Sleep? ~ What are Dreams? ~ Philosophies
about Dreaming ~ Our Three Minds ~ Common
Things that Happen During the Dream State ~
Theories about Dreaming ~ Dream Research ~
Frequently Asked Questions about Dreams

The Forgotten Language ~ Common Dream Types
~ Common Dream Themes ~ Dream Symbols ~ Dream
Archetypes ~ Remembering your Dreams ~ Strategies
for Recalling your Dreams ~ The Dream Journal ~
Questions to Ask about your Dreams ~ What to do
with your Dream Account ~ Building your Personal
Symbol Dictionary

Introduction

The Power of Dreams

We all dream. We dream every night, whether we remember it or not. We live in two worlds, the "real world," where we are conscious and awake, and the "illusionary world," where we are asleep. Dreaming comes spontaneously to us all. It is one of our greatest powers, as this book will show you.

Our dreams can affect us intensely. They can move us by their emotional and spiritual force so that we awaken in tears, or excited by an experience or an idea. We may have many sensory experiences while we dream; feeling, hearing, smelling and tasting as well as seeing visual imagery. We may even imagine, as we lie half awake, that the vivid dream experience we have just had was real.

What our dreams can tell us

Dreams are one of the most powerful means we have of communicating with ourselves, because they can allow us to understand ourselves. They act as a metaphor or story that reveals our desires, our longings and our secrets. They also convey our fears and limitations. They do this to allow us to sort out our challenges and work out our differences. They send us the message that some issues in our lives are unresolved, or offer us guidance about future events or issues.

This book can help you build your own set of dream symbols, learn your own dream language, and discover the guidance your dreams hold.

To sleep, perchance to dream.
— WILLIAM SHAKESPEARE,
HAMLET, ACT II SCENE 1

Deciphering the Message

Though our dreams are always communicating a message to us, this message is often unclear. Our dream memories are frequently foggy and fragmented. As the conscious mind tries to understand these memories and put them into sequence, they may lose their power. *DREAMPOWER* will give you practical techniques for deciphering the message from your dreams.

Messages from the unconscious mind
The mind operates on three levels:
  • The conscious mind is the doing and choosing mind – that part of the mind that does the thinking, judging and analyzing.
  • The unconscious mind is the storehouse for our emotions, habits and behaviors.
  • The higher conscious mind is our source of knowingness, intuition and openness to a higher awareness.

Dream messages come through the unconscious mind, which communicates with the self via symbols and images. In this book, we explore the interaction between the three minds as we dream and as we recall our dreams.

AN ALTERED REALITY
We do things in dreams that are often unheard of in our "reality." As we dream, we may find ourselves:
• Flying quite naturally.
• Communicating with people whom we haven't seen in years.
• Appearing younger one moment and older the next.
• Meeting up with someone who has the appearance of a stranger, yet is actually a person we know well.

Developing Dreampower

One of the mind's primary jobs is to maintain the data that has been collected during the day. At night the mind processes this information, discarding the elements that are not relevant or needed. The dream state is where we do most of this work.

Dreampower is an innate tool you can use to discover more about your dream state, and consequently more about yourself. Gaining dreampower is a three-stage process:

~ 1 Understanding your dreams.

~ 2 Learning how to communicate with your dream self.

~ 3 Controlling your waking world using messages received from the dream world.

The meanings of our dreams are complex. They reveal our individuality to each of us. You can use dreampower to unlock the secrets of your mind as you gain the gift of insight. This book offers you the opportunity to become your own dream interpreter.

Acknowledging the sources

Much of the information we have on dreams today comes from the work of many people. We are still unraveling the mysteries of dreams, but much has already been discovered. Building on these discoveries, each one of us can become proficient at understanding dreams. We can learn to program our own dreams and, ultimately, our futures.

Using our dreams to empower our lives

Using our dreampower means using the guiding principle that is buried deep within us. Learning the forgotten language of our inner world is the true method of empowering our lives. Dream language is a language that can be understood and learned by all people of all ages, cultures and levels of education. It is a truly universal language.

How to Use this Book
for Maximum Potential

DREAMPOWER will help you discover the principles of sleep and dreaming. As with many other aspects of our lives, when we understand how our dreams work we will be able to use them more effectively. This book will show you ways of using your dreams to tap into the secret forgotten power of you.

This book has been divided into four sections, each of which builds on concepts introduced earlier in the book. We therefore suggest that you read sequentially for maximum benefit.

Section 1, **The Principles of Dreams**, explains the principles of sleep and dreams and explains how the mind and brain function when we are in specific stages of sleep. We look through history at dream doctors and scientists who have uncovered the theories of dreaming for us.

Section 2, **The Language of Dreams**, helps you to explore your dream symbols and learn your own dream language – and, consequently, how to interpret your own unique and multidimensional dreams.

Section 3, **Creative Dreaming**, bids you to become a creative dreamer – to learn how to control your own dreams. Explore astral travel and profound lucid states of consciousness. Use the techniques and exercises in this section to help you program your dreams so you can find answers and achieve results in your waking state.

Section 4, **Beyond the Dream**, takes you beyond the dream state to methods used by shamans, medicine men and other spiritual healers to gain further insights into yourself. You can learn to use dream enhancers, communicate with your Dream Guides and develop your intuition. You can also experience dream sharing, and take a journey to your future self.

Principles of Dreams

In this section, we begin our exploration of dreampower by looking carefully at what dreams are, and how we experience them. We examine the way both our bodies and our minds experience dreaming. In the next section, we will learn how to use this information to understand our dreams so we can gain clarity in our lives.

What is Sleep?

Sleeping is what we do when we are not awake. It is when our conscious awareness becomes passive and the physical body slows down to rest, rejuvenate and re-energize. It does all this without the interference of the thinking, conscious mind. During sleep, the mind allows the unconscious and higher conscious minds to take control. We will suffer from insomnia if we try to sleep while our conscious minds are operating.

What are Dreams?

Dreaming occurs when a person is asleep and the mind shows black and white or colored pictures, moving or still, that relate to his or her life. When we dream, we are organizing and archiving memories and experiences. The communication of thoughts is moving naturally between the conscious, unconscious and higher conscious minds, creating dreams.

We spend a third of our lives sleeping. In a lifetime, by conservative estimates, six to seven years are spent dreaming. Each night, we dream for approximately two hours, experiencing about four or five different dreams. Dreaming occurs at ninety-minute intervals throughout the normal night of sleep. These visions last between five and forty-five minutes, and increase in length toward the time of waking.

Philosophies about Dreaming

If we spend so much time dreaming, there must be something significant about it. Research has shown that dreams can have meaning. Our dreams are messages from within, multi-layered, stemming from our deeper unconscious. They can help us in our emotional, psychological and spiritual evolution and growth. Here are some common philosophies on the nature and value of dreaming.

Dreaming:

~ **1** Consolidates what we have learned from the events of the day.

~ **2** Provides a workshop for self-repair and competency.

~ **3** Provides information to assist the dreamer with past decisions and help with new decisions and activities.

~ **4** Highlights the imbalances and unrealized potentials in our lives, and brings them to our conscious attention so that we can seek improvement.

~ **5** Encourages us to reach for our desires.

~ **6** Aids us in connecting with the guidance of our higher conscious minds.

~ **7** Helps achieve harmony between body, mind and spirit.

~ **8** Rids us of the needless thoughts, accumulated during our conscious (awake) hours, that have no significance in our lives.

The philosophies about dreaming are many, but they have a common focus: we communicate with ourselves through our dreams. Our higher conscious and unconscious minds bring data to the attention of the conscious self. On the following pages, we give a more detailed explanation of these three facets of the mind.

Our Three Minds

Dreaming is powered by our three minds, or three selves. The three minds have separate purposes, and each plays a particular role in relation to our dreams.

The Conscious Mind

The *conscious mind*, also called the intellect or objective mind, is most active when we are awake. It is the part of the mind where we think, analyze and focus. It is said that our conscious mind is our perception or awareness at any one moment in time. The conscious mind's major functions are thinking, judging, analyzing, doing and choosing. It is sometimes referred to as the Administrator, Manager or Director.

We can only hold a minimal amount of information at any one time in our conscious minds, so it is easy for the conscious mind to become overwhelmed with too much information. The conscious mind is completely fed and assisted by the unconscious mind.

The Unconscious Mind

The *unconscious mind*, also called the subconscious and sometimes referred to as the Producer, is the storehouse for memories, emotions, habits, and behaviors. It is also the repository for our past experiences, beliefs, values and identity. It creates reactions based on this stored information. It is highly adaptive, and "runs" you the best it can with the choices it has available. It is responsible for the entire body and its complex systems and chemical processing.

The unconscious mind can handle and process innumerable items of information simultaneously without becoming weighed down. It is subservient to the conscious mind, having no decision-making functions of its own. This mind is not judgmental; it only stores, sorts and filters data.

The unconscious mind pivots between the conscious and higher conscious minds. One of its main functions is to communicate directly

with the higher conscious mind. The unconscious mind receives information as intuition, then passes it to the conscious mind. Often tingling or goosebumps or hair standing up on the back of your neck will indicate the passage of these messages.

The Higher Conscious Mind

The *higher conscious mind* is the part of us that has direct contact with the "collective unconscious," or Jung's "archetypes" (see pages 30 to 32). Sometimes called the superconscious mind or the Guide, it is also believed to be our direct connection with the Universal mind, Divine or God intelligence. It is our Spirit part of ourselves. It is believed to contain the knowledge of why we are here on earth.

The higher conscious mind guides us through our unconscious mind to our conscious mind. This information bypasses a person's belief systems, and the data is sometimes referred to as "pure." It flows through what we call our gut feeling, hunches or intuition. The more we establish a connection with our higher conscious mind, the more guidance we'll receive.

The connection can be experienced through dreaming. Dreaming is our knowingness, our intuition, and the door to higher awareness.

UNIVERSAL AWARENESS AND CONSCIOUSNESS
Information moves from the unconscious to the higher conscious mind, and vice versa. It cannot flow from the conscious thinking mind to the higher conscious mind. Keeping our three minds in communication with one other and in harmony is essential; if we do so, we can dream beneficially and purposefully, and lead a balanced life.

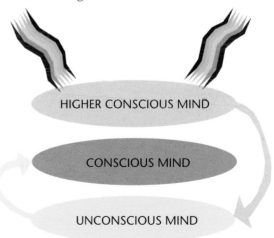

HIGHER CONSCIOUS MIND

CONSCIOUS MIND

UNCONSCIOUS MIND

13

Common Things that Happen During the Dream State

During the dream state, the following things happen:

- We have dreams, and our dreams usually focus on things that have happened recently, or are a concern to us.
- Our dreams tell a story.
- Some dreams will be in color, and some in black and white.
- Noises from outside will readily be incorporated into the dream state. For example, see the dream report below.

~ DREAM REPORT~

I was asleep, and dreaming about flying over the ocean. It was very dark, and silent, and I was afraid. Then suddenly I was listening to a song, one I'd heard before but couldn't quite place, and I relaxed. As I relaxed I began to fall, and a moment later I woke up out of my dream. I realized I had been dreaming, and the clock radio beside my bed was on. The song playing on the radio had become part of my dream.

The brain in action

The electrical and chemical activity of the brain during sleep can be viewed with an electroencephalogram (EEG), which records brain waves, and shows areas of brain activity. The brain appears to create dreams through random electrical activity. The brain stem sends out electrical impulses approximately every ninety minutes. As the left brain, or the brain's analytical part, tries to make sense of these signals, it forms a dream. The way to understand the dream best is to see it symbolically, as a literal or realistic message does not usually exist.

Our fingers, toes and genitals will often move slightly in the dreaming state, as all biological functions are active in this state. Only the eyes will move exactly as they do in the awake state.

Emotions in our dreams

At all times, the mind is communicating with the body by means of our emotions, which are transmitted through the nervous system. While we are awake, how and what we think changes the way we respond. In our dreaming state, our emotions and feelings also influence our responses.

When we dream, we experience real feeling and emotions, which are just as strong as when we are awake. If we dream when we are experiencing fear, anxiety, frustration or pain, our bodies will produce the chemicals that correspond with the emotion, just the same as if we were awake. For instance, sad images and thoughts will manufacture the chemicals of depression. Aggressive dreams will produce adrenaline, the "fight or flight" hormone.

Theories about Dreaming

In this section, we present the original theories on dreaming, and give an overview of the intensive research that has supplied us with so much valuable information about our dreams. You can also see the Suggested Reading List on page 78 if you want to develop your dreampower further.

THE FIRST DREAM PSYCHOLOGISTS

Sigmund Freud (1856–1939)

In his work *The Interpretation of Dreams*, 1899, the Austrian psychiatrist Freud said, "I shall bring forward proof that there is a psychological technique which makes it possible to interpret dreams."

Freud felt that all dreams were driven by our sexual libido. He believed that dreams are "the royal road to the unconscious": coded messages that come from the unconscious to advise of repressed desires and instincts. His hypothesis about dreams was associated with illness rather than wellness, but he paved the way for us to search our dreams for information about ourselves.

Fritz Perl (1893–1970)

An Austrian psychiatrist and one of the founders of Gestalt therapy, Perl viewed all characters and situations in our lives as disowned aspects of ourselves. He encouraged his clients to role-play and give voice in words and body language to the people and symbols in their dreams. By acting out what these elements were communicating, the dreamer could tap into the meaning of the dream and the different parts of his or her personality, and integrate them into a whole.

The Gestalt approach adds a level of consciousness to the dream state. Many people use this method today, with effective results.

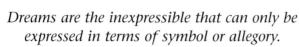

Dreams are the inexpressible that can only be expressed in terms of symbol or allegory.
— C. G. JUNG

Carl Gustav Jung (1875-1961)

A world-renowned psychologist and one-time protégé of Sigmund Freud, Jung went beyond Freud in recognizing a sub-level of the unconscious mind. He postulated that the human psyche has an impersonal level as well as the personal one.

The impersonal level, which he called the "collective unconscious," contains archetypes – remnants from the evolution of the human psyche. Jung believed that we draw on archetypes in our dreams, and the unconscious mind then individualizes them to match our specific natures. Jung believed that focusing on the symbols in a dream would reveal the dream and its conflicts to the conscious mind. He also emphasized the importance of a person's present experience to the dream.

Jung was perhaps the first to have a theory that we are dreaming all the time, and that only the distraction of our waking life leaves us unaware of the fact. He also believed that the human psyche is constantly progressing toward its goal of wholeness and maturity. Understanding and controlling our dreams – dreampower – can enable us to move closer to that goal.

Dream Research

In the late 1940s and early 1950s, dream research laboratories were established at universities and hospitals around the world to learn more about dreaming. Psychologists or psychiatrists usually supervised these activities, and observed and often controlled equipment from outside cubicles. In the cubicles, sleepers would be hooked up to an EEG and an electrooculogram, instruments that monitor brain waves, breathing and body movements.

Observers would awaken sleepers at certain times and ask if they were dreaming. This led to the discovery that there was a link between eye movement, brain waves and dreaming. This was a giant breakthrough in dream research.

People reported remembering more dreams when they were in dream laboratories than when in their normal sleeping environments. This is where the theory of conscious (creative) dreaming was first considered (see "Creative Dreaming"). According to this theory, if the mind is aware of the intention to dream and remember, then it will often do so.

REM and NREM

In 1953, it was discovered that when a sleeper is experiencing rapid eye movement (REM), he or she is dreaming. During REM, blood pressure and heart rate increase. The mind is active, yet the body has little to no movement (though some people's facial muscles and limbs will move).

For nearly one-third of our lives, we are dreaming, and most of that time is spent in REM. REM sleep occurs several times during the sleep cycle. Most people have three to five REM sleeps per night.

There are also periods of non-rapid eye movement (NREM) during sleep. These times occur when the sleeper is in a deep sleep. Although dreams occur in both REM and NREM, the NREM dreams seem to have no mental content.

The body requires both REM and NREM sleep patterns. A normal person spends about 25 per cent of the night in REM. Many factors can interfere with REM sleep, such as drugs (including prescribed sedatives and sleeping pills), alcohol, caffeine, depression, and psychological disorders.

In the early 1960s, dream researchers found that sleep and REM deprivation lead to fatigue, poor concentration, irritability and memory loss. Total sleep deprivation causes illness and mental disorders.

Recent research has shown that people suffering from serious depression dream less often than the average. As depression sufferers start getting well, they begin having more REM dreams. This is one of the indicators that dreaming is fundamental to sorting out the concerns in our lives, and assuring our well-being.

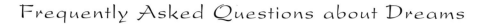

Frequently Asked Questions about Dreams

~ 1 Are all my dreams always about me?
Not entirely. We may have some premonitory and visionary dreams (see page 72) that can bear messages for other people. These types of dreams usually contain archetypal symbols, and should be interpreted symbolically rather than literally. The person in the dream who is not yourself may even have aspects of you, and this may suggest you also have areas in your life that need to be looked after.

~ 2 Do loss and grief dreams foretell a possible loss in my life?
We often have this type of dream for the purpose of releasing repressed emotions. If we don't allow ourselves to express emotions in our awake state, they will come out symbolically in our dreams.

~ 3 Do disaster dreams always precede disaster?
Some disaster dreams are premonitions, but not all. Most are manifestations of the unconscious mind as it connects to the universal awareness of the higher conscious mind. We are like radio receivers and senders, and we can often pick up information on many levels.

~ 4 Why is it that when I fall in a dream, I wake up with a jerk, as though I really fell?
This usually happens during the hypnogogic state when we return from dreaming to an awake state too abruptly. It can also happen when your body is relaxing too rapidly and you have a disruption of a conscious, or awake-type thought, that brings your body back to consciousness with a jolt.

~ 5 **What does it mean when I just take off and fly in my dreams?**

Flying dreams may indicate a creative and open phase in one's life. Many people report having flying dreams when they were children, and then losing this as adults. This could mean a block in one's openness and creativity. But to some of us, flying could also mean that our lives are out of control.

~ 6 **Why do I often dream about the need to find the bathroom?**

Finding-a-bathroom dreams are about discovering release and relief. They are reminder dreams, reminding us to let go of whatever is bothering us and not to worry about finding the perfect place or time for letting go. The act of finally going, either symbolically in a dream or by actually getting up and finding the bathroom, will feel liberating. Interestingly, it also seems you may really have to go to the bathroom when you dream about doing so.

Going to the bathroom, whether in reality or only in your dream, represents a change and a release symbolically, and sometimes realistically as well.

The Language of Dreams

The Forgotten Language

Dreams have their own unique meanings. The knowledge of these meanings can give us a real understanding of what we dream about, and of our lives as a whole. It is important that we devote some time and patience to the effort of understanding our dreamscapes, and the messages that are being sent to us via the unconscious and higher conscious minds. In the process, we can learn a new language – the language of our dreams.

This is the first step to attaining dreampower. Knowing the language of your dreams will help you open new pathways into your mind, strengthen your awareness, and liberate yourself as you realize that you are a multi-dimensional being.

WHAT'S IN A DREAM?

1 The person in the dream is present in a story or a scene.

2 The dreamer is either the subject of the dream, or a spectator.

3 The dream is in black and white, or in color.

4 Conversations can be understood by the dreamer without any actual words being spoken.

5 Dreams may be a multisensory experience, in which you can revel in the sensations of touch, smell, hearing and taste, as well as see pictures.

6 Each dream is of a specific type, and contains certain themes and symbols that tell about our nature, our preoccupations and the needs of our innermost self.

Common Dream Types

Dreams communicate to us in different kinds of ways, depending on their type. For example, an inspirational dream will teach us something about ourselves. A recurring dream will remind us that we need to work an issue out.

Most of your dreams will probably fit into one of the following categories:

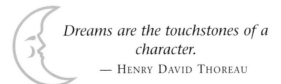

~ **1** Cleaning-the-mind dreams. These dreams sort through the emotional and mental clutter caused by whatever has been on your conscious and unconscious minds. Having a cleaning dream is like having the garbage collector take away the garbage. Think of how much junk and clutter we accumulate during the day. We input an immense amount into our minds during the day, from television, radio, the internet, newspapers, and numerous sounds and scenes happening in the background.

Don't imagine that all your dreams are cleaning dreams, however. As you begin to record your dreams, you will find out how varied they can be.

~ **2** Challenge-conquering and problem-solving dreams. These dreams can help you to tap into information and understand valuable messages. Sometimes you may feel utterly exhausted after dreams of this type.

Dreams are the touchstones of a character.
— HENRY DAVID THOREAU

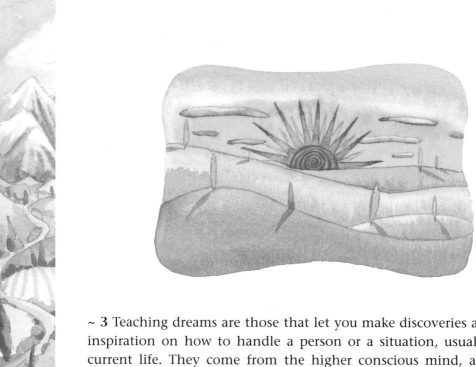

~ **3** Teaching dreams are those that let you make discoveries and receive inspiration on how to handle a person or a situation, usually in your current life. They come from the higher conscious mind, and can be greatly valuable for your waking life.

~ **4** Premonition or intuition dreams often give you some kind of fore-knowledge – a peek at something that will happen in the future. These dreams have a special feeling about them. As you learn to remember your dreams and recognize the symbols they give you, you will be able to transfer the message of your dreams to your waking life.

~ **5** Visionary and prophetic dreams come from the higher conscious mind that is connected to the soul. These dreams frequently come with insights, realizations and a sense of knowingness. They often come to help make sense of spiritual matters in our lives.

~ **6** Environmental dreams are produced when something in the environment gets integrated into the dream story – a phone ringing, a song playing on a radio, a hot room, a meowing cat, barking dogs, or a vehicle starting up. A full bladder or physical illness can also infiltrate your dreams.

~ **7** Nightmares are dreams that get our attention by saying to our unconscious mind, "There is something here you need to deal with."

We often flee nightmares before the full message is communicated. The key to dealing with a nightmare is to face the source of the fear in the dream – the thing or the pursuer. Having a nightmare warns us that something we have repressed is affecting us: that the issues we have failed to confront are issues we need to deal with now. If not dealt with, they will recur, or become waking nightmares in our lives.

We often remember our scary dreams. We often don't remember consciously what we have repressed – the thing that caused our nightmare. However, learning how to interpret our dreams will enable us to work this out.

~ **8** Recurring dreams are dreams we have often, like reruns of an old movie. Sometimes they may be serial dreams – dreams that are in episodes, or part of a series. These dreams are giving a message. They are trying to get our attention on something we haven't yet dealt with. It is most important to write down this type of dream and work out the symbols and message (see pages 26 to 31 for help with their meaning). Then the dreams will stop.

Sometimes our dreams don't fit one of the above types, but are dream fragments only. However, even fragments are important to record, as they act as a summary, containing the essence of a dream.

All the things one has forgotten scream
for help in dreams.
— ELIAS CANETTI, THE HUMAN PROVINCE

Common Dream Themes

Certain themes – events, subjects or ideas – appear in most sleepers' dreams. These themes relate to aspects of ourselves.

The themes of our dreams often correspond with the themes of our lives in our awake state. We may never experience natural disasters in our lives, or take part in an event in history, but when these experiences come up in our dreams, they may parallel events in our waking lives.

Dreams about being chased usually mean we are avoiding something. The key here is to turn around and face or confront whatever is chasing you. This will put an end to dreams of this kind.

Dreaming about death is a sign that something is ending, making way for the birth and renewal of something else. Take note of the symbols and feelings in dreams with this theme. The idea that death is required in order to ensure the growth of another may seem both sad and scary.

Dreams about disasters indicate sudden and out-of-control upheavals in your life. They often indicate turning points and opportunities for new directions. Rather than acting as bad news dreams, they reflect change.

Dreams about falling usually occur when you come back into your body too fast after a dream in which you have been astral traveling (see pages 52 to 54).

Dreams about flying usually mean you are astral traveling, or consciously out of your body. They can be liberating and fun, giving you a sense of freedom and unlimited potential. As you gain control of your flying dreams, you will be able to go anywhere you like.

Dreaming about a period in history or people in period costume can represent a past life or genealogical (ancestral) memory. Dreaming about a challenge or problem that occurred in another time or age may give you insight into an issue in your own situation.

Dreams about sex have little to do with sex itself. They usually indicate the need to integrate the male and female energies within yourself. Often, dreaming about having sex with someone may mean you are in a nurturing situation with that person, you may be merging in some way with that person, or opening yourself up to that person.

Having an orgasm during a dream is thought to act as a release and a way of restoring balance. Remember that we are all physical, emotional, mental and spiritual beings, and sexuality is a part of the self that needs to be acknowledged. Dreams are often the only way we do this.

Dreams about traveling are symbolic in terms of the direction in which you are traveling. Are you going in circles, up and down, right or left, forward or backward? *Pay attention to the direction,* and you could gain a sense of the are in which you need help.

Dreams about being lost often represent confusion, and a sense of being misunderstood. They may be full of feelings of uncertainty and apprehension. By paying attention to where you are lost (in a school, a house, a garden etc.), you could gain a sense of the area in which you need help.

Dreams about being a prisoner indicate that you are restricted in some aspect of your life, and you need mobility, or more movement.

Many other themes may arise during your dream time – for example, being unable to find the bathroom. Observing your dreams and recording them in a journal (see pages 34 to 38) will allow you to see your own personal themes, and give you much insight about the needs in your life.

Dream Symbols

Our dreams speak to us in symbols: objects, stories and pictures. Symbols are the means we have of communicating with our inner selves, a type of personal shorthand, far easier to interpret than verbal communication. Once we know our own symbols, we always get the message.

Dream symbols can be objects, things, people, scenes and colors from our lives – unexpectedly simple or ordinary objects such as houses, people, modes of transportation, food, furniture, dishes, mirrors.

They can also represent emotions, feeling, health, work, money and our beliefs about life. They come from our individual life experiences. As we think about our personal symbols, hidden meanings and truths from the unconscious mind will reveal themselves.

The personal meaning of symbols

Dream symbols have personal meanings for each of us. Dream dictionaries may be useful at times, but they may not cover our own specific meanings for the symbols that appear in our dreams as our own personal shorthand to our unconscious minds.

The table opposite illustrates a situation in which three people saw the same symbols in their dreams, but ascribed different, highly personalized meanings to them.

DREAMER	PERSONAL MEANING OF SYMBOL TO DREAMER			
	Ship at dock	Old shack on cliff	Mirror	White horse running wild
Alice	Movement away from something	On the verge of collapse and falling apart	Self-reflection or a revelation	Strong sense of being untamed, yet ultimately good
James	Great changes with regards to a passage	Old memories that are stored far away	Have a look at yourself	Pure energy surging forward naturally
Karen	Shipment of something inbound or outbound	Dilapidated ideas that are on the edge of desolation	The real me, exposure	Unbridled passion that is looking for a target

Interpreting your own symbols

If you record your dreams for some time, you can then look back and discover the meanings of your symbols. As your dream symbol collection grows, you will notice that some symbols recur. Their meanings can be different, as each dreamer has different meanings for different symbols. Alternatively, symbols may have a multitude of meanings, but a pattern will emerge, making it easier for you to interpret your dreams. For example, dreaming frequently about ships on water may reveal to one person the fact that he or she is always on a quest in life, while the same symbol may tell another of the need to move on and overcome obstacles.

Dreampower through dream symbols

Uncovering the meaning of your dream symbols may seem a complicated task at first, but the rewards will be immense. Stick to a routine to ensure regular practice, so that your interpretation skills multiply. Once you become adept, you can use your dreams to work out the challenges that face you as well as predicting what could happen in your future.

Dream Archetypes

What are archetypes?

Just as symbols personal to us and individual in their meanings appear in our dreams, so do archetypes – universal symbols. In terms of this concept, originated by Jung, archetypes are symbols that have emerged in the consciousness of humankind independent of our individual memories or levels of psychological development. They come from a universal unconscious, and are identical in all humans.

According to Jung, the archetypal unconscious is a universal memory bank that has been built up by the mental activity of humankind since the beginning of time. It exists instinctively and yet unknowingly, and is an inheritance we all bear in our unconscious minds.

Archetypes in our dreams

Archetypal figures and symbols become more prevalent in our dreams when we have times of crisis, and serve as guideposts. Archetypal dreams often occur at pivotal points in our lives and in times of upheaval. They include spiritual journeys and pursuits, often representing a search for some hidden aspect of ourselves. Having an archetypal dream will often leave us feeling as though we have received wisdom from a source not recognized as ourselves.

Common dream figures

Jung identified seven major archetypical figures that appear in our dreams.

~ 1 Wise old person or mana personality

This dream figure could be a healer, doctor, priest, magician, mother, father, or any authority figure – often a dream guide with whom we can converse and from whom we can get guidance. Jung had a mana of his own called Philemon.

~ 2 The Trickster or Antihero

This is a clown or buffoon, a figure that mocks itself. It often interrupts or disrupts our dreams, exposes schemes, and spoils dream pleasure. According to Jung, it is a symbol of transformation.

~ 3 The Persona

This figure represents the way we present ourselves to the world. It is the mask that we wear in order to deal with our waking lives. When it appears in our dreams, it often comes as a tramp or a scarecrow, a desolate landscape, or a social outcast. Dreaming about ourselves as naked represents the loss of our persona.

~ 4 The Shadow

This archetype, recognized by Freud, is defined by Jung as the thing a person has no wish to be. It is the primitive, instinctive side of us. The Shadow reveals itself as a figure with mischievous, sometimes violent and brutal actions. It feeds on fear and hate, and persecutes others. It can take the appearance of ourselves or any other person who confronts us with the things we prefer not to see, hear, feel or do. It arouses strong emotions of anger, fear and moral outrage. Jung insists that the Shadow is not evil, only primitive, and that its appearance in our dreams is a way of making us aware of our darker energies and what we may be suppressing.

~ 5 The Divine Child

This is the archetype of regenerative force that allows us to realize our individualism. As the little child, it symbolizes the true self, the same inner flame of who we were at birth and in childhood. It usually appears as a child or baby, and is innocent and vulnerable, yet in possession of a vast transforming power and understanding.

~ 6 The Anima and the Animus

These are the feminine and masculine qualities of reactions, impulses and moods. This archetype serves as a soul guide, pointing us to the areas of our unacknowledged inner potential. The Anima (female) or the Animus (male) appears in dreams as a great person or as an animal of power, strength and charisma. When we have dreams with these archetypes, it means we need to integrate the male and female within us. Seeing a combined figure in your dreams can show your development: the Anima may be a tigress, who is symbol of both aggression (the huntress) and protectiveness (the mother).

~ 7 The Great Mother

This archetype plays a vital role in the development of our minds, bodies and spirits. It is the symbolic great, powerful mother, who can appear in many forms – as a queen, a Goddess, a female wizard, and so on.

Dream guides often appear in our dreams in the form of archetypal figures.

Dreams are the facts from which we must proceed.
— C. G. JUNG

Remembering your Dreams

Remembering our dreams is vital. We need to recall them in order to learn our own dream language.

Decide that you will remember your dreams. Dreams are most easily recalled when we have the conscious intention to do so. Tell yourself, as you lie down to sleep, that you will remember your dreams and the details you require. Make a positive statement to focus your three minds.

Misunderstanding the importance of dreams

Dreams are an integral part of our life, yet we often deny that our dreams matter, or claim that we don't dream. It is a common human quality to discount the power of something we don't understand. Nevertheless, until we recognize that we do have prophetic dreaming abilities, our dreams will lie dormant to our conscious minds.

WHY DO WE FORGET OUR DREAMS?

Why do we forget our dreams? It may be that the untrained mind does not understand dreams, and therefore inhibits their recall.

The Senoi, a Malaysian tribe, are taught from childhood how to use their dreams for beneficial outcomes. By consciously managing their dreams while asleep, they get positive results in their real waking world, and handle their daily challenges more easily (see "Lucid Dreaming," pages 18 to 50). They follow this three-step precept of effective dream management:

1 Always confront and conquer the dangers in your dreams.

2 Always move toward enjoyable experiences in your dreams (e.g. enjoy flying: relax and float).

3 Always make your dreams have a pleasurable outcome.

If someone says, "I don't dream," what they are really saying is, "I don't remember."

Strategies for Recalling your Dreams

~ **1** To train your mind so it becomes unconsciously skilled, set aside a minimum of three to five nights a week for a period of three weeks.

~ **2** Set up your dream room as a place where the only thing you will do is sleep and dream. Remove books, television sets and radios – and anything else that will distract you from your sleep.

~ **3** Before lying down, state to yourself the intention that you will sleep easily and restfully as you remember your dreams.

~ **4** Have a Dream Journal or notebook, pen and light beside your bed so it will be easy to record your dreams as soon as you wake up.

~ **5** Record your dreams immediately upon awakening, if possible before you get up and move around.

The Dream Journal

The first step toward interpreting your dreams is starting a Dream Journal. This is the best way to remember and record your dreams.

Your unconscious mind uses dream signs and symbols (see "Dream symbols" and "Dream archetypes"). After at least 10 nights of dreaming (not necessarily consecutively), you will notice these symbols recurring. This will give you ample material for learning your own dream language. As you analyze and study your dreams, you will discover their central themes.

Getting started

~ **1** Give yourself a reminder as you are drifting off to sleep that you wish to remember your dreams. Keep reminding yourself about this. Eventually it will work, and your dreams will be vivid as you awake.

~ **2** Upon waking, immediately begin recording your dream in your Dream Journal.

~ **3** Date and title your dream as you begin recording.

~ **4** Write your dream in the present tense, as this will help to return you to the state and experience of the dream, and you will remember more details.

~ **5** Note down also what significant events may be current in your life. This will offers clues on what the dream was about.

~ **6** Make a note of the emotions felt in the dream, and its overall tone. Were you fearful or courageous, happy or sad?

~ **7** Go back mentally through your dream. List each possible symbol and theme (see pages 26 to 32 for help with interpreting these). Ask your conscious thinking mind what the symbols mean; then ask your unconscious mind what the message is.

When you are working on your dream, it will help to do active imaging. This means re-experiencing the dream in a meditative state as you explore it once more.

We must inquire what dreams are, and from what cause sleepers sometimes dream and sometimes do not, or whether the truth is that sleepers always dream but don't always remember; and if this occurs, what its explanation is.
—ARISTOTLE

Questions to Ask about your Dreams

Write down the answers to the following in your Dream Journal:

~1 Were you searching, playing, sad, running, alone, or in a crowd?

~2 Did you have an active or a passive role?

~3 Were you a spectator or a participant, and did this role change in the course of the dream?

~4 Were you male or female in the dream?

~5 Were you young or old?

~6 How were you dressed, and did this affect you?

Dream locations

Once you have been keeping a dream journal for at least two weeks, you may begin to notice that you gravitate toward a certain location in your dream time. The mind gravitates to sameness, and many dreamers will find there is a common location in many of their dreams. For instance, in Homer's Odyssey, the protagonist describes a dream location that he would return to time and time again.

Understanding your dreamscape

A landscape that recurs in your dreams will give you clues that can represent the current way you are living – a way you may not be consciously aware of yourself. When you remember your next familiar-landscape dream, try to answer these questions, noting the answers in your Dream Journal:

~1 Is the background landscape full of vegetation and color, of abundant life, or is it dry and withered? What could this mean?

~2 What are the homes made of? Brick, board, mud, glass, a tree, a cave? What do these types of homes symbolize to you? Are they old, new, in good order, or falling down?

~3 Are there mountains or rivers, oceans or lakes? What do these symbolize to you?

What to do with your Dream Account

~ **1** Look at the whole story, no matter how disjointed it is, and see if there are any parallels in it to your current life and situation.

~ **2** Read the list of symbols you have recorded, and make a conscious connection, asking yourself, "What do these symbols mean to me?" Take each symbol separately, then look at all of them collectively.

~ **3** Imagine you are taking each symbol to your higher conscious mind, and then allow your awareness to receive the insight of the message.

~ **4** Record the symbols in your Personal Symbol Dictionary (see pages 41 to 43), to compare their meanings here with other dreams. This will help you to find your common dream symbols.

When you consider all of these aspects, they will help you find your dream self, which is also symbolic of your waking-life self and the situations in which you are living.

We are just beginning to understand the special gifts that dreaming gives us. Our dreams will help us to find outlets for expression, and will often contain clues about important needs. For instance:

• Dreams that frighten us may mean we are worried about something that may be repressed by the conscious mind.

• Dreams that are puzzling often indicate a need for more information. Simply talking about the dream will often help us to figure out what we need.

• Vivid dreams, recurring dreams or a series of dreams that seem to progress in some way may have special messages for us. (Note that sometimes the dream's meaning may not be what we at first think, and our needs may not always be met).

Recognizing the feeling behind a dream will often reveal the meaning.

Personal Dream Journal

Date: _____

Description of dream:_____ Time went to sleep: _____

Time awoke: _____ Location of dream: _____

DREAM:

....

....

....

....

My role: Active/Passive/Observer/Participant

Key characters:

....

....

Period, landscape, environment:

....

....

Feelings and emotions during dream:

....

....

Symbols:

Dream symbol	Conscious symbol	Message

The symbols have also been recorded in my Personal Symbol Dictionary.

Summary (conclusions about my dream, messages it's giving me, how I should act on this) _____

Archetypal Dream

Sarah was on the verge of leaving her marriage. She felt very confused and guilty about wanting to leave a friendly, secure and financially stable relationship. However, she was not inspired to continue. She felt depressed and in a rut, and this was causing her anxiety.

What Sarah wrote in her Dream Journal:

I was at a party and people were all around me.

I was alone, just watching everyone having a seemingly wonderful time. I was wishing I could just ask someone to tell me what to do with my life. As I stood beside a table full of hors d'oeuvres, I noticed two people come into the room. They were an older couple who appeared to be blind, yet they got around quite easily. They seemed to have knowledge of my concerns, and understand them. Somehow I knew they were here to help me. I knew they had wisdom. I knew they had the answers.

The man came up to me and said, "What is it that you want?"

I said, "Will I ever find my love?"

The woman took my hands in hers and placed them in a big bowl full of dip, and pressed them together. She said, "Just ask from your heart."

I held my hands full with dip, and I firmly pulled them toward my heart, and as I did I simply floated up and up and up, and a voice said, "The answer is in your hands."

I woke up with my hands clasped to my chest. I felt clear and relieved, and I knew the answer at once. I knew I should be honest with my husband and leave the marriage. All my confusion vanished.

Dream Symbols: Sarah's Dream

Dream description: Party with blind people

Dream symbol	Conscious symbol	Message
Party, lots of people and activity	A lot going on, and things appear to be happy and active.	I'm there in body but not happy, and I feel alone.
Wishing someone could tell me	I am seeking answers outside myself.	No one has the answers. You can keep looking, but no one but yourself will really understand.
Two blind people	People who can't outwardly see, but know and inwardly see and sense: representing inner wisdom.	I have the answers within and I do know what to do.
Putting hands in dip	Something made by bringing two together (marriage). Hands in it means: go and feel it.	Let yourself feel what you have made with this person.
Pressing hands together	Joining, integrating.	Feelings need to be integrated.
Floating up	Ascension.	The need to rise above it all, move on.
Clasping hands to heart	Taking the self inward.	Knowing the truth in your heart.

Archetypal figures: Two wise people, outwardly blind but inwardly sighted.

(Sarah would now transfer the dream symbols to her Personal Symbol Dictionary for future reference and comparison).

Building your Personal Symbol Dictionary

Through understanding the language of our dreams, we can attain an understanding of the self. Working with our dreams and interpreting their symbols will take time, but this will be time well spent helping ourselves grow.

The unconscious mind has a sense of humor, and will often put puns and clues in your dreams. Be aware of visual puns when you are figuring out the meanings of your dream symbols.

As you record your dreams in your Journal and examine them for symbols, themes, aspects and archetypes, also record their meanings in your Personal Symbol Dictionary (see the example opposite). Keep this separate from your Dream Journal. Over time, you will discover that your personal symbols bear similar meanings in all your dreams.

To complete an entry in your Dictionary, do the following:
In column 1, write down the symbol from your dream.

In column 2, write your answer to the question, "What does this symbol mean to me?" Allow yourself to move outside the context of the dream and within yourself to discover its meaning. For instance, a snake may mean creepiness, threat, poison in your life, but could also reflect wisdom and adaptability.

In column 3, expand your awareness as you go within and see what message this symbol is giving you. Ask yourself, "What is the message from this symbol?"

While you are completing the columns, try to keep your mind quiet and relaxed. You may wish to become one of the characters or symbols, or ask a symbol what it is trying to tell you. If you come upon a dream image you can't figure out, just let it sit in your mind. The message will eventually be revealed, as inner guidance will always prevail.

Personal Symbol Dictionary

Dream description: _____ Date: _____

Dream symbol	Conscious symbol	Message
Party	Fun, people, activity	I'm trying to have fun, be happy
Food	Nourishment	I need knowledge
Unfamiliar people	Loneliness, no one knows me	I don't know myself
Dip	Flavor added	I need to add zest to my life
Two blind people	Two wise people	Positive message from both the masculine and the feminine aspects of the self
Clasping hands	Something joined together	The need to blend mind & heart
Rising up	Ascending	Going above for clarity

*Dreams are true while they last, and
do we not live in dreams?*
— ALFRED, LORD TENNYSON

Dream Symbol Interpretation

Dream theme: Being chased by a bull

Dream description: I'm in a field with a few people, none I can remember, yet we are friendly. I notice a bull in another field close by, and yet I am not concerned. Suddenly the bull is in my field and chasing me. I'm running and jumping fences and the bull is doing the same. No matter where I go, it follows. All of a sudden I decide to jump up on a house. Then the bull just disappears.

My role: Active/Participant

Key characters: A few other people and the bull

Period, landscape, environment: Time frame is now, landscape is an open field, dream is in color, lots of fences.

Symbols: Bull, fences, chasing, house

Feelings and emotions during dream: Fear, frustration, relief, clarity

Dream Symbol	Conscious symbol	Message
Bull – may be archetypal, Anima & Animus	Strength, danger	There's something solid I'm facing, maybe a barrier, maybe emotions, inner potential
Fences	Boundaries	Seeming obstacles in life
House	Structure in life	Safe haven
Chasing	Running away	I'm not facing something
Jumped up	Rising above trouble	Clarity is gained when rise above problems

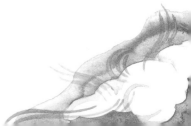

Creative Dreaming

Once you have become skilled at remembering your dreams and interpreting them, using the techniques described in the previous section, you are ready for creative dreaming. Creative dreaming is the art of programming and controlling your dreams, and communicating with your dream self. Our dreams either come spontaneously, or when we program ourselves to dream. We can program or incubate our own dreams, and then interpret them. Creative dreaming gives us techniques for enhancing our dream time and going beyond the normal dream state.

The trance state
All dreaming puts us in a trance state. This state has the same brain functionality as the sleep cycle. When we are in a sleep state or a trance, our focus is directed inwardly and the external world is limited. Creative dreaming can induce the trance state for us. This type of dreaming can take place at night during normal dream time, or during the day as we meditate, daydream or take a power nap.

The launching pad of dreaming
~1 As you descend into your dream time, take note of the images that come to you.
~2 Drift deeper with your eyes closed. Note that as soon as you pay attention to any thought, image or form, it may change.
~3 Allow the images to flow. If you are still conscious at this point, choose what dream you want to have – any type you wish.

Creative dreaming is the launching pad of dreaming. You can go beyond the "normal" dreams. You can choose to fly, to visit an old friend, to get answers to your problems, or to find peace and harmony.

Become a Powerful Dreamer

As you learn to program and control your dreams through creative dreaming, your dreampower will grow. You will be able to use all the tools of understanding and life enhancement that your dreams can give you. We can consciously decide to dream on purpose, and train ourselves to remember and interpret our dreams. Creative dreaming can enable us to use the following processes:

~**1** Dream incubation: You can program where you want to go and what you want to do, see and find out about.
~**2** Lucid dreaming: You can have conscious dreams where you make decisions and control the dream.
~**3** Astral traveling: You can travel to wherever you wish.

You can use any of these techniques deliberately in your dreams to explore, discover, recover and search the infinite. You can travel almost anywhere, and discover almost anything you can imagine:

• Travel in your dreams to the Dream Library to research and get information. Go to read books you will write in the future. Go and do research, go and talk to people whose ideas you admire.
• See the Dream Doctor to get advice or help with health issues, maintain your health, have a check-up with the best practitioners, get a physical tune-up, or have dream surgery.
• Go to the Dream Bank to organize your finances, or get financial advice.
• Visit the Dream Lovers' World to connect with your future love, to discover ways to have a harmonious loving relationship, or to forgive and be forgiven.
• Attend the Dream School to be educated on anything you are interested in learning more about.

Dream Incubation

Dream incubation is a form of creative dreaming. It was first practiced over 5000 years ago in Egypt, Greece and Rome. It is a traditional way to deliberately induce the state of a dream.

In the ancient days, the aspiring dreamer would spend the night in a sacred temple where people went for healing and guidance. The dreamer would pose a question or problem to the priests before retiring, and the next morning the priests would interpret the meaning of any dreams the dreamer had had the night before.

In our own age, we can also program ourselves to dream in a process referred to as creative incubation. This is where we ask for guidance, answers or clarity on a particular theme. We can go within to our dreams for this. In all probability, this will give us the guidance we need. With all inner dream work, intention, not ritual, is what matters.

How to incubate a dream

~ 1 In a positive and clear manner, state what you intend to find out or need help with (no beating around the bush or hidden agendas). Ask, "Should I change jobs?" or "How can I resolve this issue?"

~ 2 Write down the question or request. Think about it during the day, and when you retire, state it clearly.

~ 3 Before you go to sleep, remind yourself to remember your dream.

~ 4 When you first awaken, record the dream. Be on the alert for any striking or unforeseen events that may relate to your question or request.

*Every night we dream, and we experience
the power of creating.*

Incubating a Dream

I had been out of work for several months when I was suddenly offered two very good jobs. They had similar job descriptions: one was with a large firm, and the other with a medium-size to smaller company. I wanted to choose wisely. I decided to use dream incubation to help me with my choice. The intention was to get clarity about which job to accept.

That night I had an amazing dream. I was in a large factory, and many people were working, at an almost frantic pace, all around me. I was looking for the lunchroom, and no one would stop to tell me where it was. Suddenly, I found myself in a small conference room. Someone at the front was telling everyone about a new development. Before I knew it, I was standing there as the instructor, and on my head was a crown. Everyone seemed to be listening and enjoying themselves.

I decided to take the position with the smaller firm. The key message I got was that I would get lost in the large company, and the smaller one would allow me to shine.

Dream Journal extract

Feelings and emotions during dream: Confusion, frustration, curiosity, satisfaction, enjoyment.

Dream Symbol	Conscious symbol	Message
Large factory with many people, no one would stop to help.	It's a big world, and life is going on all around it. People too busy to stop.	Lots of things going on and happening in my life, maybe larger isn't better.
Small conference room.	A place to settle down and listen.	Realizing I can stop and listen to new directions in my life.
I was the leader or instructor, and people were listening and enjoying themselves.	I was leading and instructing, and it was easy and great.	Go for the job that could offer managerial opportunities.

Lucid Dreaming

The Dutch physician William Van Eeden first coined the term "lucid dreaming" in 1913. Lucid dreams are those in which we have conscious (thinking) awareness that we are dreaming, and we control the content and sometimes the sequence of our dreams. Some people levitate and fly in their lucid dreams.

Having a lucid dream means:
- Manipulating the dream state in the way we desire.
- Steering the dream with a conscious reaction while we are dreaming.
- Retaining awareness during the dream without awakening.
- Having the chance, during the dream, to access all memories and all of the thought processes of our waking life.
- Feeling the same as if we are awake – other than knowing that we are asleep.

Becoming a lucid dreamer
When we are dreaming, we become carried away in the dream and don't usually realize we are dreaming. Developing the ability to break through the dream state takes practice.

~ **1** Get into the habit of checking with yourself during the awake state. Ask, "Is this a dream?" Do so with regularity, and this habit will flow in to the dream state, within which you will also ask yourself, "Is this a dream?"

~ **2** As you ask the question "Is this a dream?" look at your hand. If it looks normal, then you are awake. If it appears disfigured or odd, you are probably in the dream state.

~ **3** If you begin to feel yourself returning to the awake state, start to spin your dream self upward. This will normally take you back to the lucid dream state.

Carlos Castaneda, a Peruvian-born anthropologist, claimed that he had an old Yaqui Indian guru and guide named Don Juan Matus. Don Juan took Castaneda as his apprentice in sorcery and magic. Castaneda delved into dreams and the way to have lucid dreams. One method he used for recognizing if he was dreaming or not was to ask the question "Am I dreaming?" as he looked at his hand.

Controlling your lucid dreams

When you are lucid dreaming, you can take control of the dream. Use the helpful tips below to become a master of lucid dreaming. Remember that you cannot be physically hurt or killed in a dream. The dream is an altered reality, an illusionary world that merely symbolizes our real world.

• In chase dreams, we can decide to turn around and confront whatever is chasing us. This is often the best solution. Whatever is chasing us will change as we confront it.

• In disaster dreams, we can decide to control the upheaval and find opportunities for solutions. For example, you may dream of being in a tidal wave, with a giant wave about to pull you out to sea. You could decide to create a giant boat that would let you ride the wave to safety. This would give you the opportunity to find a new land or place where you can be safe and happy, rather than terrifyingly hopeless or helpless.

Our truest life is when we are in
dreams awake.
— HENRY DAVID THOREAU

• In dreams where archetypal figures appear, we can communicate with these figures. If we wish to do so, we will need to make a conscious decision, before we go to sleep, that we are going to confront and talk to these characters. Dialogue with the dream characters is as easy as asking them what they are trying to communicate to us. Dream people are there to tell us something. You could ask, "Why are you in my dream, and what you trying to tell me?" or, "What is your positive intention about being in my dream?"

• In dreams where we are naked and uncomfortable, we can ask ourselves, "What do I need to know or change? And how do I make the alterations?"

• In recurring dreams, we can tell ourselves we are going to seek out the message, and let it transform us. An example is the movie *Groundhog Day*. Once the protagonist decided to make positive changes, he broke his recurring *déjà vu* dream, and there were positive outcomes and solutions. If you have recurring dreams, you can tell yourself you are going to find what the dream is trying to communicate to you. You can confront whatever is recurring or whatever the block seems to be. Recurring dreams only recur because they have not communicated to the dreamer whatever their intention is.

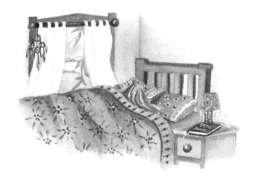

Incubated lucid dream solution: My intention was to find the lost locker dream and receive any message it had to give me.

Incubated dream: I was in the school, it was a bit brighter, and this time I had a locker number on a piece of paper. I was searching, and then I stopped in the middle of the hall and I asked, "What do I need to understand and do to find my locker?" I turned around, and the number on the paper and the locker, behind me were the same – 321. I opened the locker and it turned into a big room full of books like a library. As I went inside, it was as though I had found a room where I could find solutions and answers. That was the last time I had that dream.

In lucid dreaming, we are more than the actor. We become the writer, the director and the star of our own movies.

Our normal waking consciousness is but one special type of consciousness, while all about it parted by the filmiest of screens there lie potential forms of consciousness entirely different.
— WILLIAM JAMES

Astral Projection

Astral projection, or astral travel, means willing one's self to leave the physical body consciously and travel to other locations. Doing so requires a relaxed state of consciousness. Just as we can program our dreams, so we can program ourselves to astral travel during our dreams.

It is believed that we have a silver, or astral, cord that keeps us attached to our physical bodies on the earth plane. The cord is believed to be invisible and elastic, made of an ethereal substance. It contains the life energy, and is attached to the astral body when it is on an astral projection or travel. The cord allows travel in realms and planes beyond the physical during sleep.

There are two types of astral travel:

~1 **Pre-planned** – This is when we will the self to leave the physical body and travel to other locations. A journey can be pre-planned and pre-programmed. This can take place in a dream state, a trance meditative state or a hypnotic state.

~2 **Spontaneous** – This occurs when we have an unwilled separation of the dream mind from the physical body. This is sometimes caused by an accident, fainting, severe pain, or anesthesia. When this happens, the astral body hovers above the physical body, often quite alert as to what is happening to the physical body. It is often a surprise to us when we realize in our dream that we are astral traveling.

The mind remains active throughout the sleep state until the dreamer goes into astral projection. This is the only time the mind has a break, or total release.

How to do astral traveling

It can take a lot of practice to astral project or travel. Often, the more you try this procedure, the more elusive it may seem. The following are simple steps to help you achieve this wonderful state of dreaming.

Four steps to astral travel

~1 Relax in a safe place where you will not be disturbed.
~2 As you relax, drift deeper, using deep breathing.
~3 Consciously decide you will astral travel.
~4 Resist controlling the journey, relax, and let go.

When you realize in a dream you are in astral projection, you will also be lucid dreaming. This will sometimes cause you to come out of the dream. If this starts to happen, imagine yourself spinning upward until you are back in the dream flying or astral traveling.

Spontaneous astral projection

At the birth of my daughter, there were difficulties that led to my hemorrhaging heavily when she was six days old. I was taken to the hospital, and when they could not stop the bleeding, it was decided to do an emergency hysterectomy. During the operation, while under anesthesia, I had an astral projection dream, a near-death experience.

I was floating just above myself, looking down upon all the people in the room. There was blood all over and people scurrying around, and the mood was extremely somber. I felt light, however, extremely well, and very curious.

Then suddenly I felt myself being almost sucked upward. I found myself in a room, although it seemed to have no doors or windows, and I was with what I'd call an angel or higher being. I knew I was in the presence of a loving, kind and wise energy. I felt completely, utterly at one, peaceful and loved – as if I had come home. We were talking about my life, what I had come to do and the gifts and blessing I had, when the angel suddenly said, "Do you want to stay, or do you want to go?"

I could have stayed; it felt so completely wonderful there. But I knew I had to decide – I couldn't just stay in limbo. I asked if I could go and ask my husband. The next thing I was aware of I was floating outside the window of the 5th floor of the hospital, and looking in at my husband. He looked very worried and sad. When I got his attention, I asked him, "Should I stay or should I come back?"

He looked at me and said, "It's up to you."

My next awareness is of waking up in the hospital bed the next day feeling physically miserable, but incredibly spiritually transformed, and inspired. This was a major turning point in my life.

And that's not the end of the story. My husband had the experience of seeing me floating outside the hospital, and remembered my asking him if I should go or stay.

Dream Mapping

Writing dreams to empower your life

We often find we are consciously reviewing things that we are anxious about. This can cause us to have spontaneous dreams. And, when these dreams occur, we can use them to get clarity and assistance. We can also use them to start the process of dream mapping. This means incubating a dream, and then becoming lucid during the dream.

Two ways to use dream mapping

You can wait until you have a dream about a situation. Then:

~1 Remember the dream, write it down, and interpret the symbols.

~2 Decide to incubate a dream to go back and have the experience the way you'd most like it to be.

~3 Remember the incubated dream, and write it down.

~4 Translate the symbols, and interpret the dream to determine its meaning.

Alternatively, you can incubate a dream, making the experience happen as you want it to. This can be done during your night's sleep, or for a meditation or a daytime visualization.

~1 Design the dream, and visualize yourself having the experience the way you want it.

~2 Incubate the dream.

~3 Remember the incubated dream. Write it down.

~4 Decipher the symbols, and interpret the meaning.

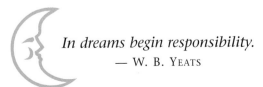

In dreams begin responsibility.
— W. B. YEATS

Meditation to Expand the Dream Connection

Read these instructions onto a tape recorder. Play the tape to activate your dreams consciously during the meditation state. Then, as you sleep at night, you will dream and remember.

~**1** In a quiet place, get comfortable. Sit or lie with feet and arms uncrossed.

~**2** Close your eyes, and experience the feeling of relaxing and going deeper. Notice the differences in your body, your mind.

~**3** Let yourself follow the flow of images that come as you drift deeper. As soon as you notice any image, thought or form, it may change.

~**4** Allow the images to flow in and out. Notice that you can choose to have any kind of thought you wish.

~**5** You can choose to go beyond "normal" dreams. You can choose to fly, to see an old friend, to get answers to problems, to find peace and harmony.

*"Only the dreamer shall understand realities,
though in truth, his dreaming must not be out of
proportion to his waking!"*
— MARGARET FULLER

~**6** Now relax, and breathe slowly and deeply.

~**7** Imagine you are drifting, going deeper and deeper, and your brain is switching dominancy. Your unconscious mind is now in control, and your conscious mind is passive.

~**8** Expand your awareness to encompass yourself, the room, the place where you are sitting, the building, the block, the city, the state, and so on. Let this awareness expand and grow.

~**9** Connect to this awareness, and let a symbol, a gift from within, form and come into your space, your imagination, your inner vision.

~**10** Breathe, and feel the peace, tranquility, harmony, balance and oneness. Accept the gift.

~**11** Note how you feel about this gift, this space, this place. Imagine how you can use this in dream-time awareness.

~**12** Start to come back. Do it slowly and easily, becoming aware of here, of now. Open your eyes and wiggle your toes to ground yourself, and return.

Dream Meetings

You can set up a date with another person while you are both dreaming. With practice, this technique can be easy. The dreamers incubate the dream individually, but have common themes for their dreams.

~ **1** Decide on a date and time for dreaming together.
~ **2** Agree on where in dreamland you will meet (any place you both know).
~ **3** Focus on your intention to meet as you begin dreaming.
~ **4** Let the dream begin.
~ **5** Record your dream in the usual manner.
~ **6** Later, talk to the other person as soon as possible to compare dreams.

Special notes
• The intention is most important. If only one of the dreamers takes the dream meeting seriously, it probably won't work.
• Sometimes you may dream of the same location, but find yourselves at different points in the same area.
• You may or may not be conscious of astral traveling.
• Once you master dream meetings, you can meet anywhere in the world.

Dream Meeting

Two friends, separated by a job transfer, decided to experiment with meeting each other in a dream meeting.

Diane and Susan: "We decided to meet in our dreams on a set date at our favorite outdoor cafe. We decided we would sit outside and have a coffee and a normal chat."

Diane: "I woke up and was amazed that I had had a most wonderful visit with Susan. She was waiting for me. She had on sunglasses and a blue and white striped top. I found myself suddenly sitting down, and we had a bottle of wine and just laughed and talked."

Susan: "I woke up very excited as I remembered my dream with Diane in detail. She arrived in a taxi and came running up to me at the table. The table had a red and white stripped umbrella and there were two glasses already on the table. George, our favorite waiter, was there and he opened a bottle of champagne or wine and we had it and giggled, laughed and had a great long visit."

Dream Sharing

Dream sharing, or talking about your dreams with others, is a powerful way to discover meaning from your dream messages. Sharing your dreams can expand your dreampower immeasurably. The differing perspectives of other dreamers can give you more knowledge, and offer you an assortment of insights that can provide a rich foundation of understanding and self-discovery.

Setting the process in motion
Sharing your dreams means sharing information about your most intimate self. Select as your dream-sharing partners those with whom you share trust, respect, honesty and understanding.

Facilitate the process by using a simple ritual to set out the space in which sharing will takes place. Choose a comfortable area. Ensure that you will be undisturbed. Bring your Dream Journal and Personal Symbol Dictionary with you if you need to prompt your memory.

The rewards will be gratifying.

Shamanism and Dreams

In some cultures, people share their dreams with the shaman, a psychic and seer. A shaman is a tribal wise person, healer of body, mind and spirit. The shaman's skills are either natural or learned.

There are shamans in most cultures and countries: Alaska, Canada, the Continental United States, Hawaii, Mexico, Central and South America, Asia, Siberia, the Ural-Altaic region, the Orient, Australia, New Zealand, and Africa. The shaman's title may vary from culture to culture. He or she may be known by titles such as Medicine Man, the Holy Man, Kahuna, a Spiritual Counselor, Sibyl, Magician, a Wise Woman, Herbalist, and more.

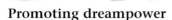

Promoting dreampower

One of the major tools of the shaman is to teach how to remember, understand and create dreams. The shaman can also get psychic insights from other people's dreams, as well as his or her own. In both of these ways, the shaman's important task is to help others learn how to use their dreams in order to achieve a more empowered life.

See yourself in others, then whom can you hurt? What harm can you do?
— DHAMMAPADA

Beyond the Dream

Once you are adept at creative dreaming, there are many advanced techniques you can use to take your dreampower to new heights. Several methods are outlined in this section. When you are doing creative dreaming – controlling and programming your dreams – you can use these methods to achieve an advanced level of dream awareness, and gain further guidance and insights into yourself.

With the insights our dreams have given us, we can go beyond the dream to explore further. In this section, you will learn how to:

- Utilize natural elements like crystals.
- Develop harmony and balance as you work with your chakra system.
- Go beyond the lucid dream as you write your dreams to empower your life and set up your goals.
- Explore your future self and future world through the dream world.
- Connect you with your higher self and Mother Earth, as you stand outside the normal arena of reality.

At this stage of your exploration and awareness of dreaming, you will be well aware, while in your dream state, that you are in fact dreaming. You will notice many differences between your awake and dreaming states. The table gives a few examples.

AWAKE STATE	DREAM STATE
Ground feels solid.	Ground changes feeling, appearance.
When running, can start and stop simply.	Running becomes slower, faster or frozen.
Things change normally, in sequence.	Things change randomly and illogically.
Jumping means going up and down.	Jumping means going up, and then flying.

Using beyond-the-dream techniques, you can become aware of even more differences between the awake world and the dream, and of ways to make your dreams themselves more rich.

Dream Enhancers

For some, dreaming haphazardly is not good enough. Our forefathers and shamans (see page 60) of both distant ages and the current day have used dream enhancers to enrich their dreams. Dream-catchers, crystals and chakra clearing are some of the effective devices.

Crystals

Crystals are natural, perfect amplifiers and transformers to influence your physical, emotional and mental energies during the awake and sleep states. They can help you to create abundance and happiness in your life, promote good health and relationships, and more.

Crystals can be carried in your pocket or purse, placed beside your bed or meditation spot, or kept under your pillow. For dream work, it is advisable to keep the crystals beside your bed or under your pillow. You could even hold them in your hand during sleep or meditation.

When selecting a crystal, choose one to which you are drawn. If you acquire a crystal that is not described in this book, then find out its purpose and utilize it in the way it best supports you.

Keep your crystals clear and clean by putting them outside on a moonlit night, then washing in salt water (do not use detergents), and anointing and rubbing with rose oils.

Dream Crystals

NAME	COLOR	FUNCTION
Amber	Golden/honey	Regenerates, increases energy levels.
Amethyst	Purple	Promotes healing, natural harmony and well-being.
Citrine	Yellow/orange	Revitalizes the body, and releases stress, tension and pain.
Clear quartz	White, clear, mostly transparent	Gives clarity, draws out the negative, stores and amplifies feelings.
Diamond	Clear	Gives focus, direction.
Lapis lazuli	Dark blue	Heals the emotions, gives courage and strength.
Peridot	Light green	Releases negative programming.
Pyrite	Gold	Clears frustration and traumas, balances awareness.
Rose quartz	Pink	The love stone; creates and enhances love and harmony.
Ruby	Red	Promotes the healing of heart matters and maintains balance in the body.
Tiger's eye	Black, yellow	Protects, grounds.
Turquoise	Turquoise	Protects, opens throat chakra, guards against adversaries.

Crystal Dreaming Technique

This can be used as a dream or meditation enhancer.

~ **1** Choose a crystal that relates to the concern or challenge on which you wish to work.

~ **2** Go to a place where you normally sleep or meditate. Ensure you feel safe and comfortable and are not going to be disturbed.

~ **3** Hold the crystal in your hand, or place it near you.

~ **4** With your eyes closed, go within, and center yourself by focusing on a point in front of you and above eye level.

~ **5** Expand your awareness to encompass the whole of you, from the top of your head to the tips of your toes. Imagine a bubble or cocoon all around you.

~ **6** Ask for help with whatever your concern or challenge may be.

~ **7** Holding the stone or concentrating upon it, imagine as you take deep breaths in that you get clarity and balance as you drop the question in the stone.

~ **8** Let the question go, and begin floating back down to now (if you wish to return), or deeper into your dream-time sleep.

~ **9** When you return to the waking state, you will be refreshed, and unconcerned about the outcome, knowing things are working out.

~ **10** Record your dream, including any images or symbols.

~ **11** Now ask yourself how you feel about the concern or challenge you used to have. See if you feel different, and have any insights.

Dream-catchers

Many American Indian tribes have used dream-catchers. They are usually circular, made from rawhide, and look a bit like cobweb. They hang above the sleeping area to filter out unnecessary dreams, and catch dreams that we should remember. Dream-catchers are in plentiful supply at most New Age stores. They are useful, and well worth a try.

65

Chakras and Dreams

Seven basic energy centers exist within each human being, called chakras. The term "chakra" comes from the ancient language of Sanskrit, and means "spinning wheel" (imagine the energy spinning in a circular motion). Each chakra relates to a particular stimulation or energy point. These points store suppressed and unresolved memories from our current lives, our genealogical (ancestral) life and our past lives.

Using chakras, you can work on your feelings and problems without having to know where the problem started. This is particularly helpful in cases in which the concern may have originated from a past life, a genealogical memory or an early childhood emotion or memory you cannot recollect.

Chakra Name	Color	Part of the body	Unresolved issues and feelings suppressed in the chakra
1 Base or Root	RED	Coccyx	Physical & material limitations, anger
2 Creative	ORANGE	Abdomen	Shock, trauma, avoidance, fear
3 Solar plexus	YELLOW	Mid-trunk	Indecision, forgiveness, sadness
4 Heart	GREEN	Heart	Compassion, understanding, love, pain, hurt
5 Throat	BLUE	Throat	Communication with self and others, guilt
6 Third Eye	INDIGO	Between the brows	Blocked memories, inability to accept the present, hopelessness
7 Crown	VIOLET	Top of head	Negativity, insensitivity to others, unconnectedness, numbness, worthlessness

Chakra Dream Technique

You can use the chakras in dream time, by concentrating on a particular chakra or group of chakras before dropping off to sleep. The purpose of this technique is to bring into balance your energy centers where unresolved and negative emotions and issues are stored. It is advisable to begin with the base chakra, and to use the technique on each chakra in turn as you work up to the top or crown chakra.

Once this is done, you can then explore and clear your unresolved emotions and issues. Doing so will effectively assist you in aligning your conscious, unconscious and higher conscious minds. This will give you more awareness in your dreams. Once this state has been achieved, the mind and body will be relaxed, and receptive to the information gathered. When we relax, we are separating the external (outer world) from the internal (inner world). This is why relaxation is such a significant aspect for all inner work such as meditation, hypnosis and dream time.

~1 Concentrate on a chakra point in your body. Imagine you can see the chakra. Note its color. Sometimes this will seem murky or muddy.
~2 If the color is muddy, begin to clear the chakra by filling it with more vivid color.

~**3** Tell yourself you are going to sleep, and you are going to dream while you sleep in order to get clarity on and help with any negative emotions or issues.

~**4** Hold in your mind the image of the color in the region of the chakra as you allow yourself to drop off to sleep.

~**5** When you awaken, recall your dream, record its description and events in your Dream Journal, make note of any symbols, and interpret the meaning.

~**6** Sitting quietly, close your eyes and see how you feel about the emotion or feeling you used to have. Imagine what the color of the chakra looks like now.

Once your chakras are clear, they will spin in balance and work together with ease, and your life will improve. Clean and clear chakras should be bright, and full of rich, vibrant color. See the chakra chart (page 66) for the corresponding emotion and color.

~ DREAM REPORT ~

Chakra Dream

I was having fearful thoughts during the day about almost everything. When I visualized my chakras, my solar plexus chakra was dark brown. I decided to concentrate on that area of my body. Just before I went to sleep, I imagined my solar plexus area as vibrant, and bright yellow. Here's my dream account when I woke up.

I dreamt I was dragging a ball and chain around. I was afraid and unhappy. I kept thinking all the old thoughts, full of foreboding, and everything in the dream was in black and white. All of the sudden this tiny little yellow sun crept out of my pocket. Then I remembered the chakra, and I took the sun out and it grew and grew as I held it in my hands. I felt the dream world become colorful and bright. Then I woke up, and felt unencumbered and happy for the first time in a long, long time.

Grief Dreams

It is advisable to take control of your grief dreams. Like all other dreams, they are there to help you. Use your dreampower to understand them, overcome the grief, and continue living your life.

Basic principles for dealing with dreams that are sad and unpleasant:

- Record them in your Dream Journal.
- Have a look at the symbols that emerge.
- Use lucid dreaming to communicate with whoever is in the dream, and ask for clarity and understanding.

~ DREAM REPORT ~

Grief Dream

My husband had died two years earlier, and I was grief-stricken. I couldn't shake my grief – until I had the following dream.

I was watching a parade with many people marching down the street. They were all carrying candles. I knew I was looking for someone. Suddenly, I saw my husband. He was smiling, and looked well and happy to see me, but his candle was not lit. This concerned me deeply.

I found myself standing next to him. I was troubled that his candle was not lit. When I asked why, he communicated to me that my tears kept putting the candlelight out.

I awoke to an amazing knowingness. I felt different, and knew I wanted to let him go, to bless him, to thank him for the time we had had and to release this sadness.

Something we were withholding made us weak,
until we found it was ourselves.
— ROBERT FROST

69

Dreams and Death

Dreams come from a source that is deeper and wiser than the everyday waking mind. If we pay attention to them, they will give us answers and stretch our understanding. In times of crisis, they can provide immeasurable comfort.

Dreams can have a particularly powerful meaning for the dying. People who are near death often have profound dreams. Their dreams – like all other dreams – are highly symbolic, and will communicate what they need to know. Using this vital information can enable the dying to complete and close their lives, and make the transition from this world to the next peacefully.

Being able to talk about dreams or visions is therapeutic for people who are dying. It will help them to understand their concerns. If someone you know is near death and has death dreams or visions, he or she may be struggling with something that is difficult to understand. Encourage people in this situation to tell you the details, and help them to interpret their dreams. See "Dream Sharing," for more about sharing dreams.

Anyone who is extremely ill should pay particular attention to recurring and vivid dreams. Sometimes, there will also be a series of dreams that are unfolding or progressing. Also note that:

• A dream that is puzzling often indicates a need for more information.
• A dream that is frightening may relate to fears about the illness or about dying.

70

• A dream full of frustration and anxiety may mean that the dying person is worried about family, arrangements, and the expense of the illness.

Sometimes, a death dream may come to someone other than the dying person. Once this dream is understood, it can give understanding and assistance to the dying person and the loved ones.

~ DREAM REPORT ~

Death Dream

When my brother was in his early thirties, he was dying. The family was devastated. He fought his illness as hard as his body allowed, and hung on for at least a year longer than was expected. Dying didn't seem to be the option he wished to take. While he was going through the torment of his illness, I had a dream.

I could see my brother in an above-ground swimming pool. He was in it up to his chest, and trying to get out. There didn't appear to be any water in the pool, and he was leaning on the side holding out his hands. My mother was crying and trying to lift him over the side, and they were both exhausted.

The family was all gathered around, just watching and crying. When both he and my mother decided to rest and it seemed he had no bodily strength left, he simply put his hands together and lifted himself straight up. He looked serene and peaceful, and the weight of the experience lifted with him.

I awoke crying. The symbolism was profound, and so were my feelings.

The next day, I was told he had passed over.

This dream was a metaphor for how he had struggled against death and how my mother was shattered, and how they both would not give up. Once my brother was released, his letting go was peaceful and beautiful. When I now think of my brother, I can still see his serene face with that peaceful look.

Premonition Dreams

We sometimes have premonition dreams – dreams that predict future events. Often these require little effort to interpret. Below is a description of some famous premonition dreamers.

Abraham Lincoln dreamed his own death. In his dream, so reports say, he was wandering around the White House following the sounds of "pitiful sobbing." Every room he went to looked familiar, but no one was there. He then entered a room to see a corpse laid out, its face covered, its body wrapped in funeral vestments. When he asked the mourners who was dead, he was told, "The President, he was killed by an assassin." A loud burst of grieving from the crowd awoke him from the dream. He told his wife about his dream. A few days later he was assassinated.

Elias Howe was perplexed by a detail as he worked on his invention, the modern sewing machine. He was not sure where to position the eye of the needle.

Then he reportedly had a dream in which a tribe captured him and danced around him with upraised spears, threatening to kill him unless he finished his invention. He noticed something very odd about the spears: they had eye-shaped holes near their tips. Upon waking, Howe realized that this was the solution: he needed to put the eye of the needle near the tip.

Albert Einstein claimed that the theory of relativity came to him while he was in a twilight state of consciousness. (Today we'd call it a power nap.)

General Norman Schwartzkopf was reportedly guided by his dreams in the Gulf War.

Robert Louis Stevenson was a prolific dreamer. In his book *Across the Plains*, he related how entire stories would come to him in his dreams. He taught himself to remember and incubate his dreams. He would concentrate on a fantasy before going to sleep. One of his dream-inspired creations was *Dr. Jekyll and Mr. Hyde*.

Developing Intuition in Dreams

Here is a half-hour meditation to help develop dream intuition. Use it just before dream incubation, or any other dream work. Record it for yourself, reading slowly with long pauses, and then play it back.

~1 Sit with your back straight and your feet on the ground, legs uncrossed.

~2 Take deep breaths, and let your diaphragm expand as you feel yourself relaxing.

~3 Hold your breath for a moment and then slowly exhale, letting all the air out. As you do this, let out all negative thoughts, all sense of limitation you may have been holding on to.

~4 Now imagine there are holes in your feet letting you take in great big breaths of air from the center of the earth. Let the earth's energy come up through your feet, legs, hips, arms, shoulders, heart, throat and all the way to the top of your head.

~5 Let the breath linger there as you fill yourself with this earth energy – all that you need to connect and balance you.

~6 Now imagine a tiny ball of light just above your head, your crown chakra, getting brighter and brighter.

~7 Connect with this energy as you breathe it in. See it as a beautiful ball spinning with all the colors of the rainbow.

~8 This is the energy from the collective pure unconscious. All that there is to know, to learn, to be, is here now.

~9 Let yourself be filled with the energy, wisdom, guidance and clarity you need. Connect with your intuition, allowing the two energies to meet somewhere in your body and connect to make you whole.

~10 Bless these energies, this wholeness, and this power.

~11 Let yourself float up as a mind and not a body to a place of peace and safety.

~12 Now relax, and let yourself go higher and higher. Rest. Wait at least three minutes here before you continue.

~13 Gently start to return down to your body, taking your time, and now down to the room. Hear the sounds around you, feel your body, and come back.

~14 When you are ready, wiggle your toes and move your feet to ground yourself.

Dream Guides

A Dream Guide is a figure that appears to us in our dreams, to give us an understanding of our lives. It is something outside of ourselves, rather than the higher conscious mind, which we experience in our dreams as a sense of knowingness. The Guide appears in human or perhaps animal form. Be open to what your Guide may look like, and compare it to the seven archetypes that Jung describes (see the discussion of archetypal figures on pages 30 to 32).

We all have Dream Guides. Some believe we have different Dream Guides for different situations in our lives. By programming yourself prior to your dream state, and declaring that you will be aware of Guides, you are opening the way for the appearance of your own Guide. Continue to be both open and patient, and you will not be disappointed.

Whenever Guides reveal themselves to you in your dreams, attempt to communicate with them. If you should encounter any figure you feel bad around, ask for it to identify itself. Trust your feelings. You can dismiss anything that does not serve you. Spirits on a lower plane can come in if you have not protected yourself. It is important to ask only for your true Dream Guides to come to you in your dreams. Dream Guides cannot lie to you about their identity.

Make it a nightly ritual, before you go to bed, to say a prayer or protect yourself with light. This will enable you to have the best possible experience with your Dream Guide. Not only can you establish a rapport with your Guides, you can also explore the dream world with their help, and learn more about yourself.

Meeting your Dream Guide
~ **1** Set your intention to have the Guide appear in your dream.
~ **2** Protect yourself with a gold, white or pink light, to keep out lower spirits that may wish to bother you.

~ **3** As you are getting comfortable and relaxing, allow yourself to imagine ascending to a place that brings you comfort and peace – a favorite mountain, the moon, the stars, or even somewhere you have not physically been in your waking state.

~ **4** Record your dream when you awake, taking special note of any characters in your dream – people or animals, real or make-believe.

~ **5** If you communicated with these characters during the dream, what did you find out about them?

~ **6** Make a decision to invite your Dream Guides back to another dream session. Don't be surprised if, as you get to know them, they reveal their names and their connection to you. You can begin having a relationship with them for guidance and wisdom in your life.

~ DREAM REPORT ~

Dream Guide Dream

I was walking alone through the forest. I knew I was looking for something or someone. Suddenly, I saw a cave behind a waterfall. I was drawn to it, and found myself standing in the entrance. A big bird like a hawk or eagle came swooping in and landed on a rock ledge. As we looked at each other, it was transformed into a person with a long white robe. I asked who it was, and it said, "I am your Dream Guide."

Suddenly we were transported to another place, and the Guide was pointing out to the ocean and telling me my destiny lay over water.

I moved to Australia, and now travel and teach all over the world.

This is the first of many occasions in which I have used a Dream Guide to explore and find guidance.

Meeting your Future Self in Dreams

Sometimes we dream about the future. Are these "wishful-thinking" dreams, or are they foretelling our future? They may not be premonitions, but they can show us what we are drawn to.

These kinds of dreams may help us to understand:
- What is important to us.
- That we may be exerting too much energy on something that isn't worth it.
- That we may need to take another path.

> ## ~ DREAM REPORT ~
>
> ### Seeing the future
>
> I had been worried about an illness that wouldn't go away. I had had several diagnoses, and tried many remedies. In a dream one night, I decided to incubate a solution or resolution to it all.
>
> I was having a dream about singing on a stage. It was like I was observing myself, not really there. Then I realized, I was looking at an older me. It was incredible. I thought, this is an opportunity to ask myself some questions. I remember the older me told me to keep on going on the path I was focusing on as it was right. She said to enjoy work and stop living for tomorrow, as soon enough it would be here. I had to take life less seriously, and if I stopped trying to control everything, my illness would go away.
>
> I awoke to a feeling of wholeness, and knew the meeting had been real. I determined to take my own advice – and my illness left me.

Exploring the future

What if it were possible for you to incubate a dream in which you could meet the future you, and explore possible futures? Imagine going into your dream time to see how your life would be if you stay on your current path. Imagine being able to get a glimpse of how your life would be if you changed anything in it. Try the exercise that follows.

When you meet your future self, you will find the ultimate guide: your older, wiser self.

Meeting Your Future Self Exercise
STAGE I

~ **1** Create a mental picture of the "you" you are now. Visualize this in as much detail you can, and with intense feeling. Once this process is completed, leave the image for a moment.

~ **2** Next, imagine going back five years and seeing how you looked then. Note the differences in your life, your environment, your behavior, your abilities and your beliefs. Note how much you have changed, and possibly how far you have come, compared with that time. Leave this imprint there for a moment.

~ **3** Now, imagine yourself in the future, five years from now. Take note of what you'll be like if you continue on your current course without making any alterations. Note how you feel about this future you. Leave the imprint there.

~ **4** Now, call forth your ideal future self, the one that has made modifications and changes and created the ideal self that you want to be. Don't think about how to do this, just imagine it. Then step into this "you" and let yourself experience how good it feels, and make an imprint of this future you.

STAGE II

~ **1** Imagine you are still standing in the future. Look back at your present self, and ask the future "you" what is needed to take you to this future as fully as possible. Ask what you need to let go of or to change, and what you will need to start doing now in your life.

~ **2** When you return to the awake, conscious state, record your answers, and interpret your symbols.

Reading More about Dreams

Bethards, Betty, *The Dream Book,* Element Books, Rockport, MA, 1995.

Castaneda, Carlos, *The Art of Dreaming*, Harper Collins, London, 1993.

Castaneda, Carlos, *Tales of Power*, Simon & Schuster, New York, 1974.

Donner, Florinda, *Being In Dreaming*, Harper, San Francisco, 1991.

Drury, Nevill, *Creative Visualization*, Lansdowne, Sydney, 2001.

Flanagan, Owen, *Dreaming Souls*, Oxford University Press, Oxford, 2000.

Fontana, David, *The Secret Language of Dreams*, Pavilion Books, London, 1994.

Freud, Sigmund, *The Interpretation of Dreams*, Allen & Unwin, London, 1965.

Gackenbach, Jayne & Bosweld, Jane, *Control Your Dreams*, Harper Perennial, New York, 1988.

Garfield, Frank, Stewart-Garfield, Rhonda, *Dreams*, Lansdowne, Sydney, 1995.

Garfield, Patricia, *Creative Dreaming*, Ballantine Books, New York, 1974.

Garfield, Patricia, *The Healing Power of Your Dreams*, Simon & Schuster, New York, 1991.

Gawain, Shakti, *Creative Visualization*, New World Library, Novato, California, 1995.

Goodwin, Malcolm, *The Lucid Dreamer*, Simon & Schuster, New York, 1994.

Hobson, Allan, *The Dreaming Brain*, Basic Books, New York, 1988.

Jung, C. G., *Dream Analysis*, Routledge, 1984.

LaBerge, Stephen, *Lucid Dreaming*, Ballantine Books, New York, 1985.

Purser, Jan, *Meditation*, Lansdowne, Sydney, 2000.

Van De Castle, Robert, *Our Dreaming Mind*, Ballantine Books, New York, 1994.

Voigt, Anna, *Simple Meditation*, Lansdowne, Sydney, 2001.

Wolf, Fred A., *The Dreaming Universe*, Simon & Schuster, New York, 1994.

Glossary

archetypes symbols that have emerged in the consciousness of humankind, independent of our individual memories or levels of psychological development. They come from a universal unconscious, and are identical in all humans. Examples: figures, customs, myths.

ascend in dream terms, suspend one's body, climb upward, rise to a higher level of consciousness, free from the law of gravity.

astral body a spiritual double of the human body, able to leave the body at will connected to the body by a silver cord.

astral projection willing one's self to leave the physical body consciously during a dream and travel, or go to other locations; requires a relaxed state of consciousness.

dream guide an etheric (non-earthly) being who appears in dreams and brings guidance and help to the dreamer.

dream incubation method used to induce a dream deliberately. The dreamer makes a request for guidance before falling asleep, and then the dream brings the answer.

dream mapping programming one's dreams through dream imcubation so that the dream experience facilitates change in the real (waking) world.

electro-oculogram (EOG) an instrument that records the movements of the eyeballs while a person is sleeping.

electroencephalogram (EEG) a biofeedback machine that detects and amplifies the electrical impulses that the human brain emits.

intuition a non-thought that bypasses the thinking process. The information is often not logically known; it occurs spontaneously, coming from the higher conscious mind through the unconscious and is fed to the conscious mind.

lucid dreaming a dream where the dreamer is aware that he or she is dreaming.

mana personality a wise person or figure appearing in a dream to give guidance. Thought to be a prototype of the ideal human, that manifests itself in angel form.

non-rapid eye movement (NREM) type of eye movement during sleep, when the sleeper is in a deep sleep (compare rapid eye movement).

rapid eye movement (REM) the eye movement experienced when we are dreaming.

symbol an impression, word, picture, sound, taste, smell, object etc. that bears a resemblance to, or implies, something else.

transcend to rise above, go beyond, go into higher realms.

This edition published by Barnes & Noble Inc.,
by arrangement with Lansdowne Publishing Pty Ltd

2002 Barnes & Noble Books

ISBN 0 7607 3174 8

M 10 9 8 7 6 5 4 3 2 1

© Copyright 2002 Lansdowne Publishing Pty Ltd

Commissioned by Deborah Nixon
Production Manager: Jane Kirby
Text: Laureli Blyth
Illustrator: Penny Lovelock, additional illustrations by Sue Ninham,
  Jane Cameron, Tina Wilson, Priscilla Nielsen and Bettina Hodgson
Cover Illustration: Penny Lovelock
Designer: Avril Makula
Editor: Avril Janks
Project Coordinator: Bettina Hodgson

Set in Stone and Present on QuarkXPress
Printed in Singapore by Tien Wah Press (Pte) Ltd